Saint Fiacre's Garden Guide

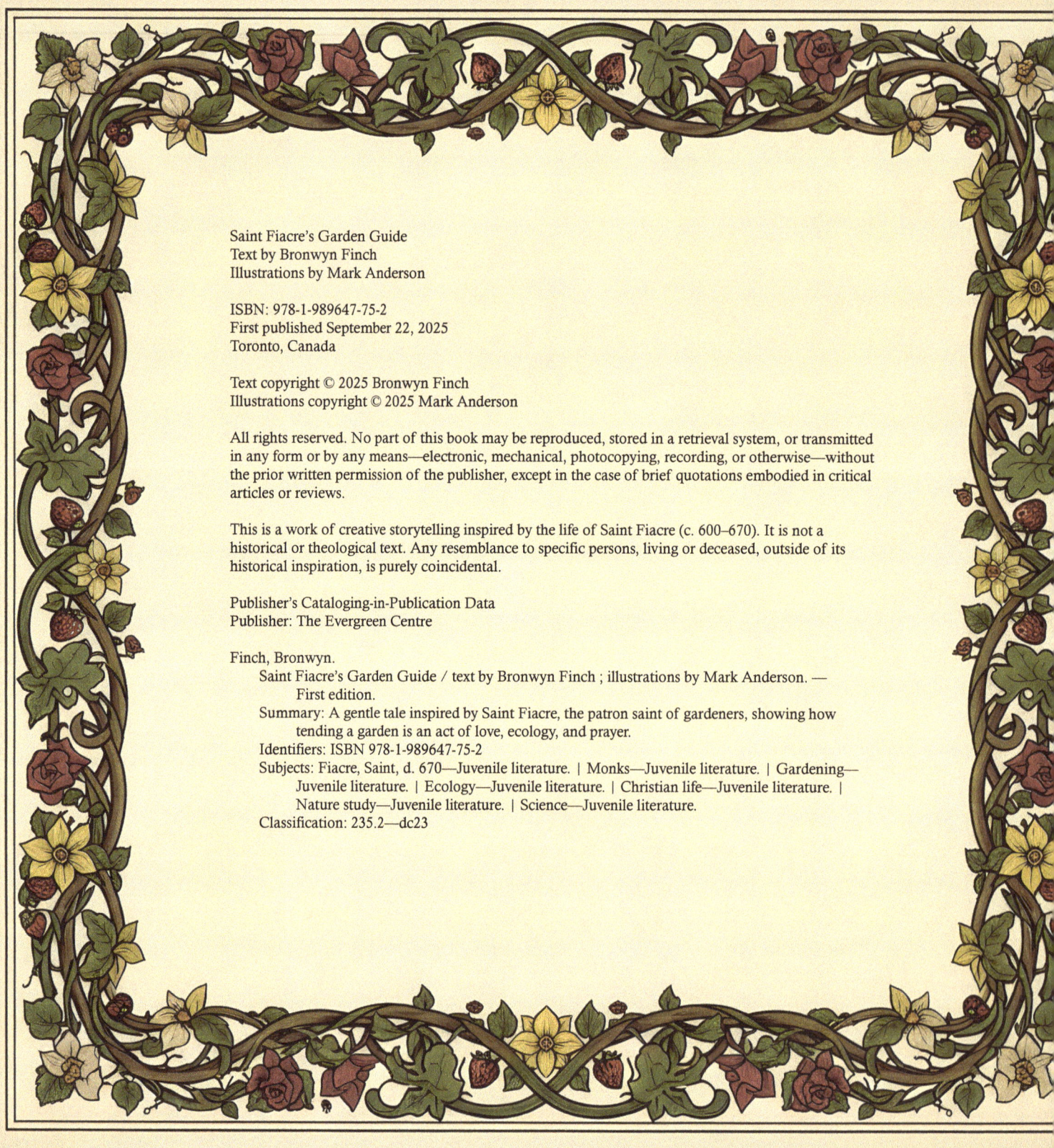

Saint Fiacre's Garden Guide
Text by Bronwyn Finch
Illustrations by Mark Anderson

ISBN: 978-1-989647-75-2
First published September 22, 2025
Toronto, Canada

Text copyright © 2025 Bronwyn Finch
Illustrations copyright © 2025 Mark Anderson

All rights reserved. No part of this book may be reproduced, stored in a retrieval system, or transmitted in any form or by any means—electronic, mechanical, photocopying, recording, or otherwise—without the prior written permission of the publisher, except in the case of brief quotations embodied in critical articles or reviews.

This is a work of creative storytelling inspired by the life of Saint Fiacre (c. 600–670). It is not a historical or theological text. Any resemblance to specific persons, living or deceased, outside of its historical inspiration, is purely coincidental.

Publisher's Cataloging-in-Publication Data
Publisher: The Evergreen Centre

Finch, Bronwyn.
    Saint Fiacre's Garden Guide / text by Bronwyn Finch ; illustrations by Mark Anderson. —
        First edition.
    Summary: A gentle tale inspired by Saint Fiacre, the patron saint of gardeners, showing how
        tending a garden is an act of love, ecology, and prayer.
    Identifiers: ISBN 978-1-989647-75-2
    Subjects: Fiacre, Saint, d. 670—Juvenile literature. | Monks—Juvenile literature. | Gardening—
        Juvenile literature. | Ecology—Juvenile literature. | Christian life—Juvenile literature. |
        Nature study—Juvenile literature. | Science—Juvenile literature.
    Classification: 235.2—dc23

Greetings, young friend of the earth!

I am Fiacre, and my heart finds its greatest joy amidst the quiet wonder of a garden.

Come, let us discover together what a garden truly is: a sacred patch of earth where we lend our hands to the miraculous unfolding of life.

Behold the rich tapestry of a garden, from the grand estates to the humblest plots!

Here, crimson apples hang heavy upon ancient branches, golden sunflowers stretch to meet the sun, and hidden treasures like crisp carrots rest beneath the soil.

What marvels do your eyes first alight upon?

Every mighty oak, every fragrant rose, begins its journey as a tiny, slumbering seed – a miniature world of promise held within a fragile shell.

What tender awakenings do you imagine these hidden gems require?

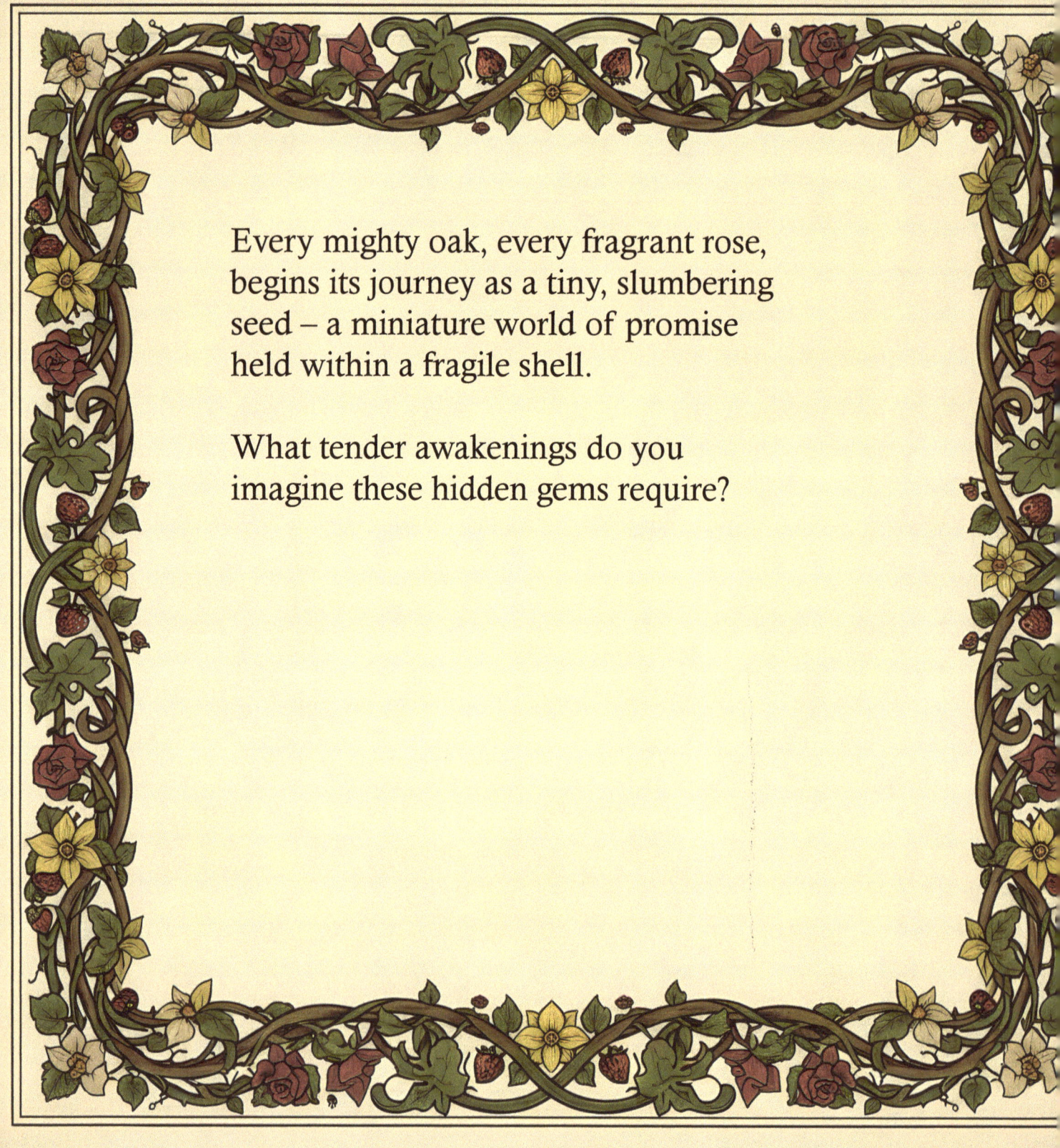

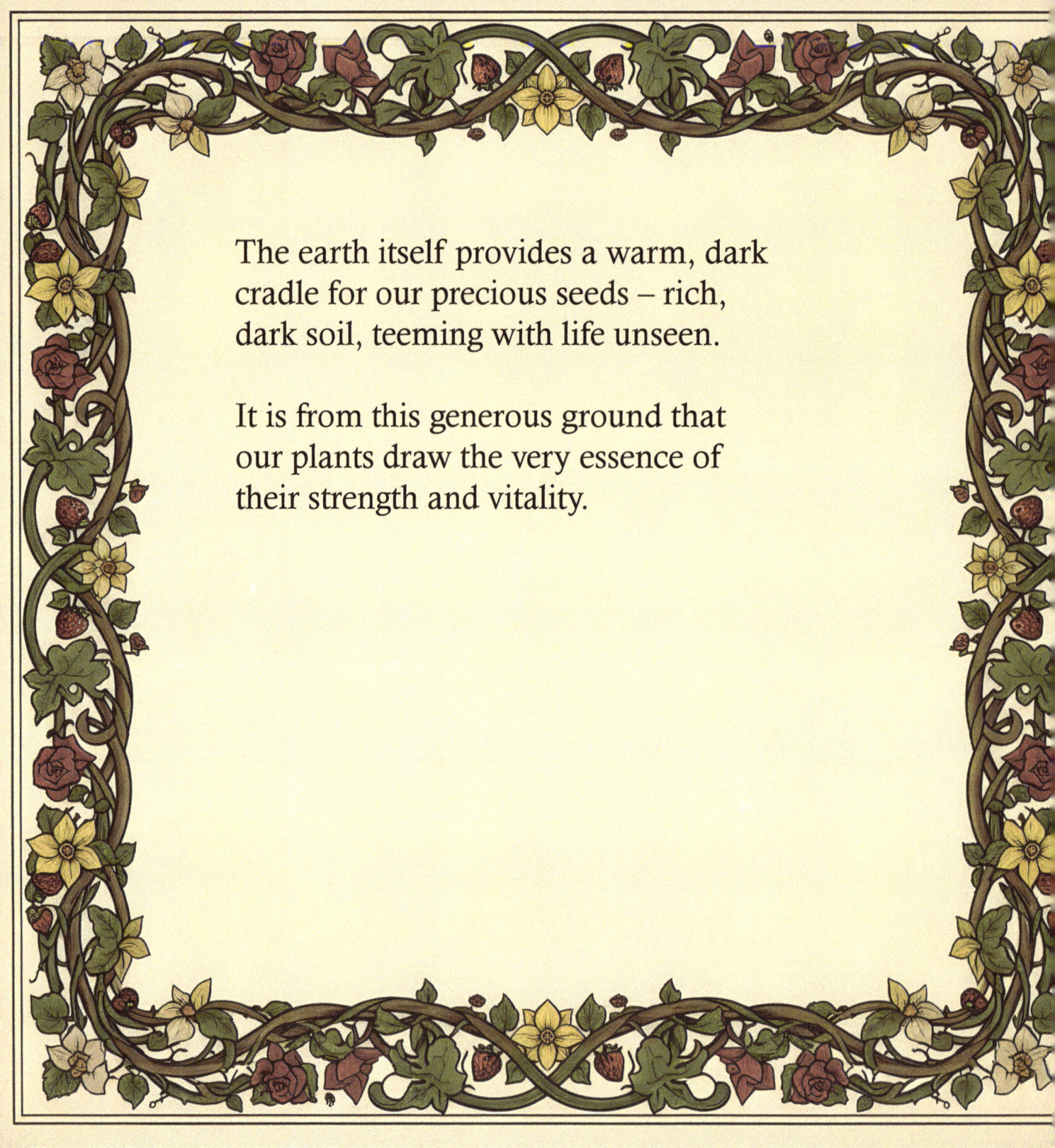

The earth itself provides a warm, dark cradle for our precious seeds – rich, dark soil, teeming with life unseen.

It is from this generous ground that our plants draw the very essence of their strength and vitality.

Just as we thirst for a cool draught on a summer's day, so too do our plants yearn for the life-giving waters.

With gentle hands, we offer them fresh, clear drops to drink, nourishing their tender roots.

The sun, our great celestial painter, bathes the garden in its golden warmth.

Each leaf turns skyward, drawing forth the wondrous energy that fuels its growth, a silent, daily miracle.

Feel its gentle touch upon your skin; it is the same warmth that awakens the plants.

Behold the bounty of our kitchen garden!

The vibrant carrots, sweet beneath the earth; the plump, sun-ripened tomatoes bursting with flavor; the cool, crisp lettuce leaves.

Each a testament to the earth's generosity.

Which treasure calls to your appetite?

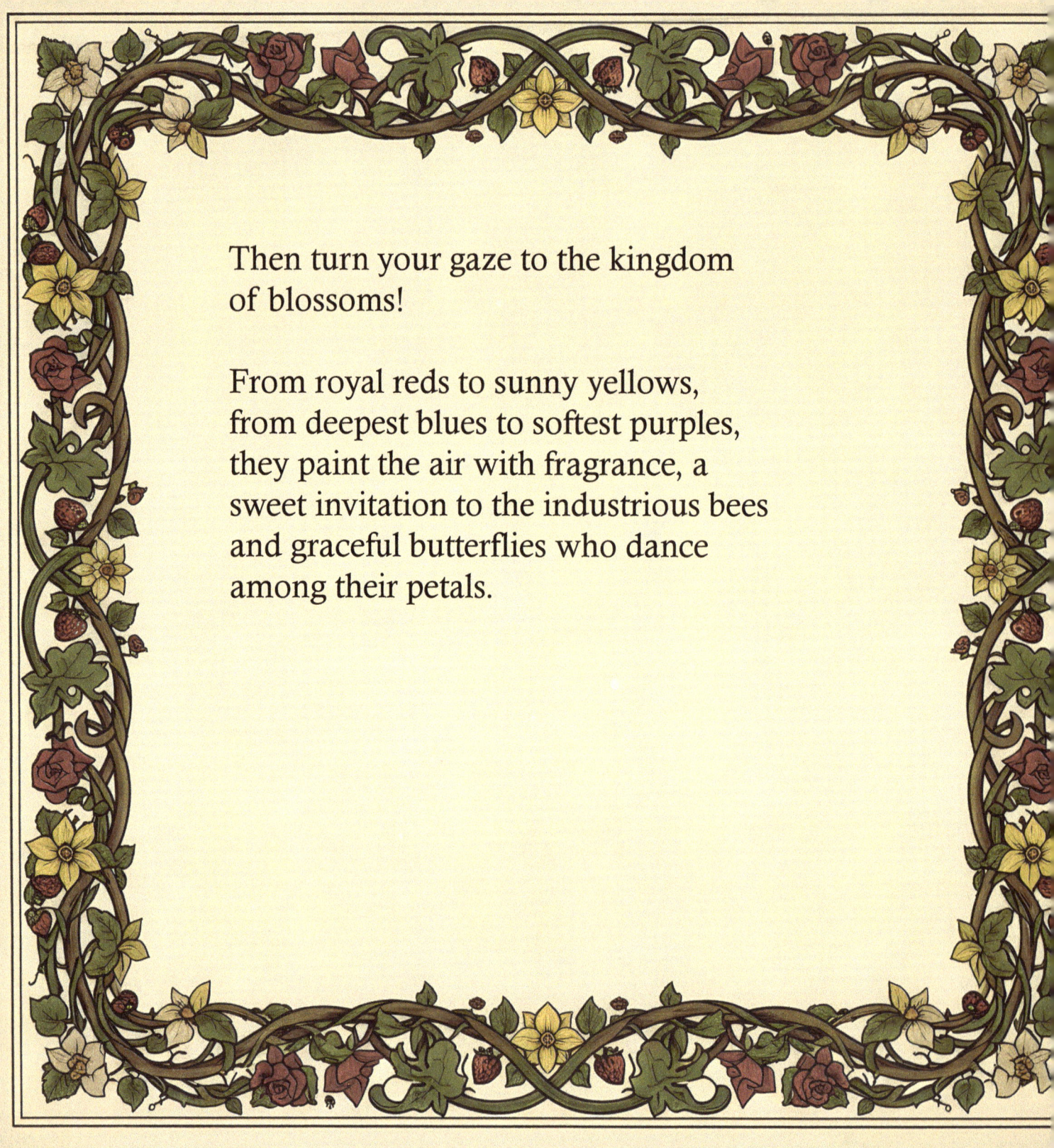

Then turn your gaze to the kingdom of blossoms!

From royal reds to sunny yellows, from deepest blues to softest purples, they paint the air with fragrance, a sweet invitation to the industrious bees and graceful butterflies who dance among their petals.

We are never truly alone in the garden, for it teems with silent partners.

The diligent earthworms, unseen artisans, tunnel through the soil, enriching it with every twist.

The tireless bees, cloaked in gold and black, flit from blossom to blossom, ensuring new life for seasons to come.

Can your eye discern these humble, vital helpers?

At last, the time of harvest arrives!

When the fruits hang heavy and the flowers bloom in their fullest glory, we gather the sweet rewards of our labor.

What greater joy than to share this abundance, these gifts of the garden, with those we cherish?

Remember, even the smallest vessel can hold a grand vision.

A single pot upon a sunny sill can become your very own secret garden.

Will you embark on this quiet adventure, nurturing one tiny seed to its wondrous bloom?

Farewell, dear companion of the garden!

May you always carry the quiet wisdom learned amongst the growing things. Remember, each tender leaf, each vibrant blossom, is a small miracle unfolding before your eyes.

Keep vigil over their growth, and may your gardening days be filled with peace and discovery!

About Our Saint:

Saint Fiacre (Fee-AH-kruh), venerated as the patron saint of gardeners, is a figure whose quiet devotion and profound connection to the earth have inspired generations. Born in Ireland in the 7th century, Fiacre was a man of noble birth, but he chose a life of solitude, piety, and communion with nature.

Seeking a hermitage where he could dedicate himself fully to God, he journeyed to France. There, he was granted land by Saint Faro (FAH-roh), the Bishop of Meaux (MOH), in a dense forest called Breuil (BROY). Legend tells that Fiacre asked only for as much land as he could enclose in a single day. When he touched the ground with his spade, the forest trees miraculously fell, and the earth opened, allowing him to easily clear a vast area for his hermitage and garden.

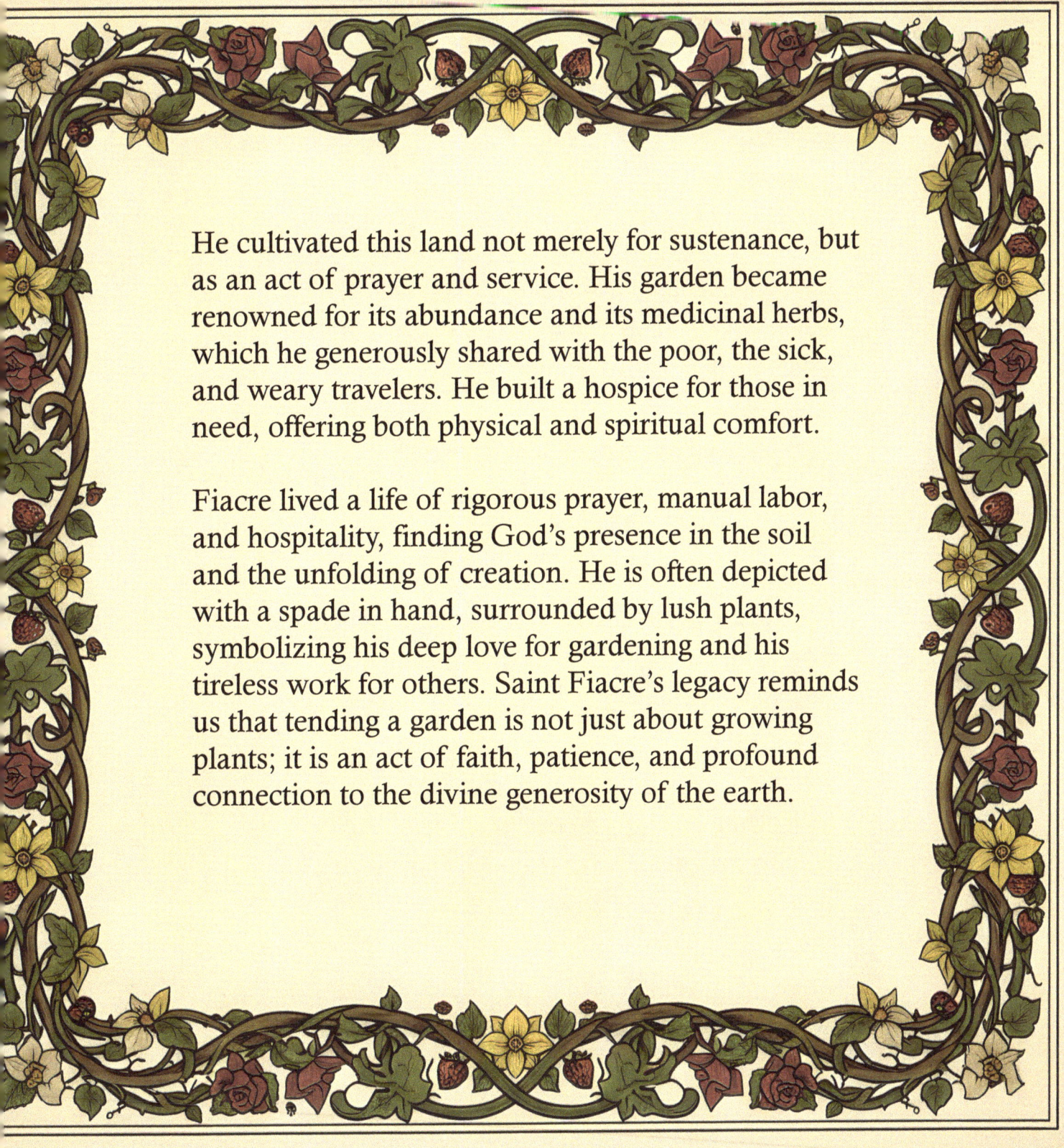

He cultivated this land not merely for sustenance, but as an act of prayer and service. His garden became renowned for its abundance and its medicinal herbs, which he generously shared with the poor, the sick, and weary travelers. He built a hospice for those in need, offering both physical and spiritual comfort.

Fiacre lived a life of rigorous prayer, manual labor, and hospitality, finding God's presence in the soil and the unfolding of creation. He is often depicted with a spade in hand, surrounded by lush plants, symbolizing his deep love for gardening and his tireless work for others. Saint Fiacre's legacy reminds us that tending a garden is not just about growing plants; it is an act of faith, patience, and profound connection to the divine generosity of the earth.

Different Vows, One Garden

Brother, your hands are truly blessed in this garden, but your path has not yet led you to the tonsure. Why does your hair remain long?"

"My vows are as a Lay Brother, Father. I dedicate my life to the labor of our community—the garden, the kitchen, the craft room. The tonsure is the mark of a Choir Monk or Priest, bound by a different commitment to daily scripture and Mass. Yet, we both walk toward the same perfection.

Whether in the chanting of the choir or the quiet turn of the soil, the work is always one of love.

Saint Fiacre's Bountiful Harvest

Saint Fiacre's garden was a miracle of quiet devotion, nurturing both body and soul.

From the fertile earth came sturdy cabbages and sweet carrots, providing nourishment for the hungry. For the spirit, he cultivated beauty: humble roses unfurled in quiet grace, and tall, elegant lilies whispered of heaven's light.

Even the little Irish robin perched on the basket handle, a cheerful witness to the bounty. In Fiacre's garden, every root and every bloom reminded him that from a simple seed, God's love and sustenance sprang forth.

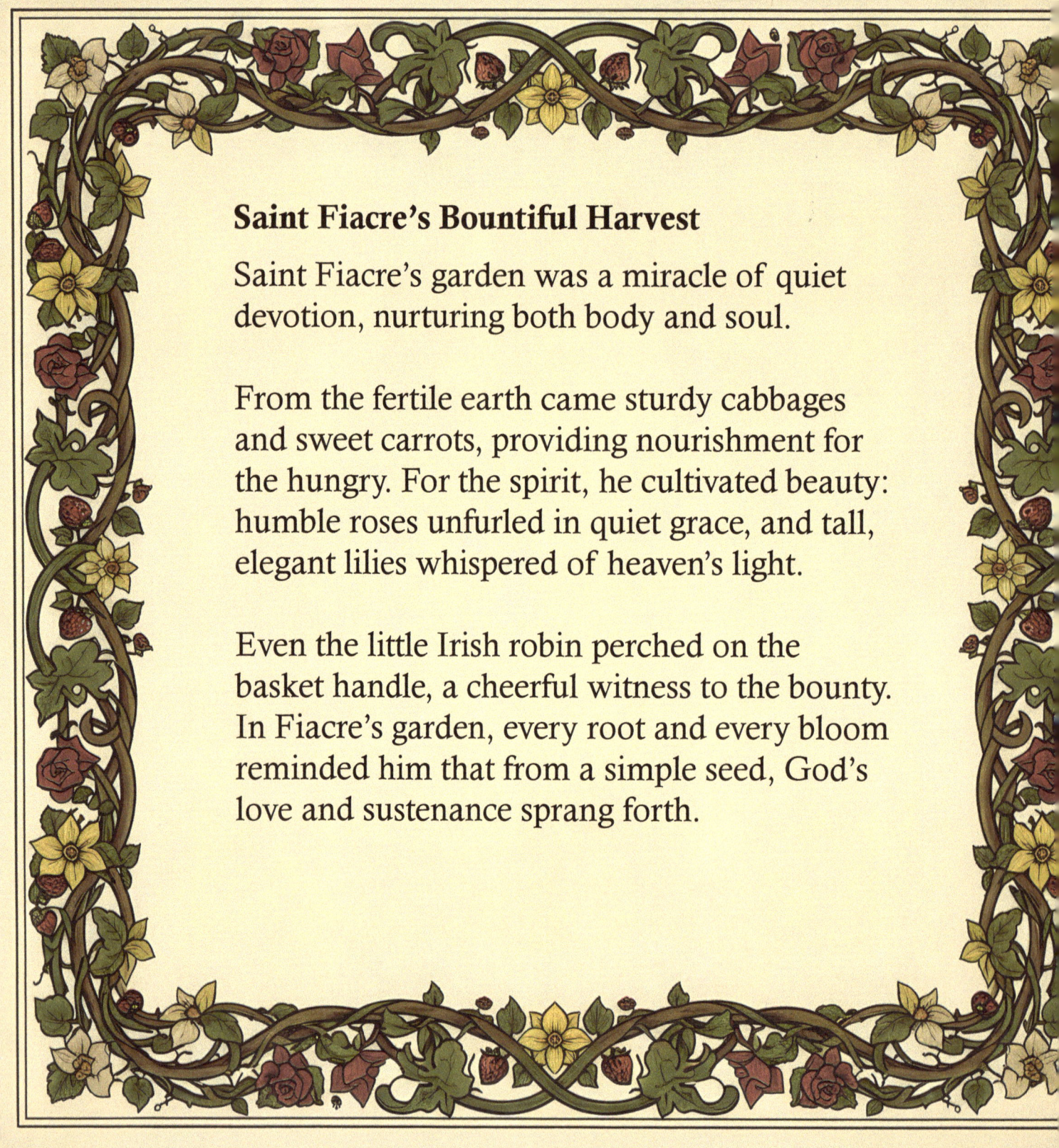

The Earth's Best Friends: Hidden Helpers

Saint Fiacre learned the secret to rich soil was trusting the hidden helpers inside the compost pile.

Think of the earthworm as the garden's little recycler. It spends all day eating up dead leaves and old food scraps. When the worm is done, what comes out is called castings.

Worm castings are like a vitamin mix for your plants, making the soil dark and soft.

Worms also dig tunnels deep into the soil. These tunnels let air and water reach the plant roots easily.

The lesson is simple: When you feed your compost, you feed the worms. The more worms you have, the happier and healthier your garden will be!

The Busy Buzzers: Bees

Do you ever wonder how one little flower turns into a tasty tomato or a crunchy carrot seed? That's where the bee comes in!

Bees are looking for a sweet treat called nectar inside the flowers.

While they drink, a yellow dust called pollen sticks to their fuzzy little bodies.

The bee then flies to the next flower and brushes the pollen off, helping the flower make a seed or a fruit. This is called pollination.

If the bees didn't move the pollen, we wouldn't have many of our favorite foods!

A true gardener plants flowers for the bees first, knowing that the bees will then help the vegetables grow, too.

Growing Deep

"Be rooted and established in love."
(Ephesians 3:17)

The Lesson:
A plant with deep roots can stand firm when the wind blows and the rain pours. Our faith is like those roots! When our faith is deep, we can stay strong when things are difficult.

Practice:
Sit quietly and think about God's love. Ask Him to help your faith roots grow deeper, like a mighty oak tree.

A Gardener's Prayer

Dear God,

Thank you for the miracle of the garden.

Thank you for the seeds of life, the helpful worms, and the busy, buzzing bees.

Help us to grow strong roots of faith, like the mighty trees.

Help us to share your love and kindness with everyone we meet.

May our hearts be as open as the soil, ready to receive your grace and grow beautiful things.

Amen.

Final Benediction

May your heart be like good soil, ready to receive the seeds of kindness and faith.

May your hands be blessed as they work the earth, tending to both the small plants and the mighty dreams.

And may the peace of the garden follow you always, rooting you firmly in love and encouraging you to grow toward the light.

Go in Peace. Plant with Joy. And, grow deep and strong in Faith and Love.